THE YUMS

Can you see Leek's
grass skirt?

She likes swishing it to and fro

Sometimes
she swishes it so high

her undergarments show

Leek just loves to dance

It keeps her in peak
condition

She would like to find
a partner

for the
'Tricky Dance Competition'

She once tried
dancing with Spud

and ended up
covered in mud

She once had
a waltz with onion

but dancing gave
him a bunion

Leek had wanted to
partner Mango

who was brilliant at the Tango

but his Mum
who calls him Mangosteen

won't let him out
'til his bedroom is clean

Leek and Strawberry
gave it a go

Ow! she kept treading
on her toe

But as soon as Leek
saw Harricot-Vert

She knew they were
the perfect pair

For the dance competition Leek put on fake tan

and Harricot-Vert dressed as Superman

They danced the twist
and the modern jive

hoping the judge would
score them 'five'

As the crowd all cheered
Leek thought it was heaven

and she couldn't
stop smiling
when the judge shouted

'SEVEN'

Created by Mary Ingram

Read about Leek's friends ...

www.theyums.co.uk

Printed in Great Britain
by Amazon

77482669R00018